ROW YOUR FUCKING BOAT

CONFESSIONS OF A NOOB WRITER
WRITING A NOOB BOOK

By Za-ar Twist

If it is a sophisticated writing technique or Magic that
you seek, seek elsewhere.
If it is drama that you expect, by all means ~
AVANTI TUTTA!

"Row, row, row your boat
Gently down the stream
Merrily, merrily, merrily, merrily
Life is but a dream"

They say the beginning is always hard.
Respectfully - they, whoever they may be, have no idea.
Either that or they were born prodigies.
They be another league. We don't mess with those.

Allow me to be quite straightforward on this one - everything is hard. The beginning, the middle, the end and everything in-between and even the in-betweens from the in-betweens, if that makes sense. Every. Thing. Choosing every god damn word, every god damn coma, every god damn stop and so on and so forth.

But the ideas - by far, are the most horrible.
Like pure torment! They come and go like rebellious teenagers facing a new existential crisis while wondering whether they should bang behind the bush on the right side of the road or the one on the left!

To all teenagers out there, sorry dudes, I too know that life decisions can be a pain in the ego.
...
But this is not about teenagers. Let's begin with the beginning.

PHASE 1

It all starts when you decide you want to tell the world
a story.

In your head images are playing one after another,
characters develop themselves creating a breathtak-
ing universe around them, everything feels in place, it
feels intense, sometimes even to the point that you
might even start laughing or crying by yourself
impressed by their unyielding tragic fates or by... you
know, whatever makes your boat float. Sometimes
this happens in public and you realize people look at
you and wonder what kind of expired weed you
managed to smoke before you left your house?
Sometimes they might even approach you and ask
for your supplier's name.

And you laugh. Oh, like a lunatic you laugh. Well, your inner self laughs - **WARNING*** - I strongly suggest you don't release your inner self in public in times like these. Depending on the country you live in, you might find yourself driven into a... Sanatorium? Or worse.

Aaaaaanyways, you keep your head up high, and your nose even upper in the sky, because you KNOW what these puny little ants don't. Not yet at least. You KNOW how everything unfolds in this new Universe that even though it might not have a name yet, someday it will place a big stamp on the entire history of literature or cinematography or the game industry.

You dream big. Dreams are free and unlimited. And it's so easy to lose your way around them.

So what do you do?

You take this even further, obviously. You start fantasizing, imagining how the Internet will be filled with fan arts of your ever so unique, ever so mesmerizing and addictive characters. You imagine yourself reading fan stories picturing relationships between characters you would never agree with or relationships that fit so well they will make you squeak and jump in your chair wondering how come you didn't think of that first?

Your head is spinning, you feel ecstatic.

With great effort, you pull yourself out of this euphoric vision of what undoubtedly must be **the Future** and bring your feet back to the present. You have work to do, right? You suddenly feel busy, important, your life has meaning, nothing else matters except this ultimate goal and you decide you will do whatever it takes to bring this project to life (*probably the stage when you also reflect upon your being and realize that holy mother of macaroni! – you might have what it takes to become this century's new Jack the Ripper if anyone should dare stay in your path!! * Please refrain from such urges if you do, I really don't want to be held responsible for this kind of revelations.*).

PHASE 2

You decided you want to tell the world your story. Right? Easy enough. Wrong.

After this, you'll spend days thinking of how you should plan, from where you should start - a lot of thinking, probably doing zilch or close to zilch. Research is mandatory, you trust; abusing the all-know/all-wise Master Gogu *(also known by the name of Google)* you manage to find some articles and armed with a stack of hope and 2 stacks of enthusiasm you conscientiously start studying: how to build a great plot/ how to create a great protagonist/ how to instigate curiosity in your readers/ how to publish on Amazon/ how to become a millionaire selling books... whoops, this deviated a bit.

Let's go back to being serious.

Seriously speaking though, we are not doing this just for money, right? Or not entirely **just** for money.

Right?!

Who am I kidding...

That's one bad thing.

And secondly, all that search will spoil, if not completely ruin, your mood. It's just so much out there. So much information. So many people sharing so many thoughts, experiences of so many things you should do or not do, things that work or don't work with examples and contradictions and reasons of why one's method is better than the other's.

YouTube videos, books, blogs, articles, step-by-step tutorials, Wikihows.

It's just too much to filter through.

There are millions of people with access to the internet and their minds can and will generate millions more of ideas. And if you don't know what resonates with you, it will become overwhelming. And no one wants to feel overwhelmed. We all like to lie to ourselves that we are in complete control of our miserable lives! <3

What to do then? Well, by the authority invested in me by the Association of Me, it is my humble belief that reading as many books as you can and writing bullshit as often as you can - might be the best practice you can hope to have. I mean to take my example, see how much bullshit I can type right now? I can hardly believe it myself.

As a side note, take comfort in writing bullshit. Nowadays you have a fair chance to get famous for that, rather than for medium quality shit.
It's a matter of taste.
And trend.
Stupidity makes people laugh.
And we need a good laugh in this depressive age.
Know what I mean? -wink wink-

As for high quality shit, you need to fail a lot to get there, I know this much. I know no shortcut to make it easier unless you're... but we don't talk about prodigies.

Don't turn into a small brainwashed/ stressed out machine obsessed with following the typology of some specific article you once read, and you thought for yourself this sounds so good it MUST BE

TRUE!

Recently, I kept bumping into numerous *"modern tutorials"* that claim to offer guidance on how to write a successful book. Basically, they advise you to abandon your originality, because no one gives a shit about your original two cents. Instead, what you need to do is go stalk some high ranked authors and just do what they do. Write what they write. If possible, write the improved version of what they write.

I'm not sure if it's just me, but to me it sounds utterly wrong. I mean, am I missing something here? Do we like know 456 Shakespeares, 2415 Mozarts and 3054 Picassos?

I mean – Yes. I am aware. Times changed. If you want to make some fast money this might actually work, otherwise… what the actual heck?

Following guidelines might help if you don't take them by the letter.

Writing is about being free. So be free, dammit! God knows it's one of the very few types of freedom that you can afford.

Alas~

The clock is ticking, time is passing.

Eventually, you get annoyed, or you forget your idea, or you get another idea that you think is better than the previous one and then you start planning from 0 again.

Then you finally decide planning is not your thing because you keep changing your ideas or because you're a rebel and it just doesn't work, OK?! You don't have to explain yourself to anyone! The public is not your mum!

Going with the flow suddenly sounds like a bliss~ YAH! That's it! Sure, you're just going to start writing! Something! Anything! And wherever this takes you, you will enjoy the ride! - *insert here motivational quotes and a flower-power mood lifting victory dance just because you can –*

**Dancing is quite healthy and quite stress-relieving, strongly encourage often use of it-

PHASE 3

And then...

Then you find yourself sitting in front of a blank page.

You got this brand new tank of paper about the right thickness *(assuming you handwrite, yeah, I know, I like to pretend I still live in the middle ages and I am actually a reincarnated witch who witnessed too many humanity horrors and now wants to write the chronicles of each of them at the light of a candle using a pen dipped in my own blood while whispering curses under the guidance of the full moo... wha'? Uuuuh...This can go places. Don't judge me! I'm an arTwist!)*.

You sharpen your pencil, you get a nice cup of coffee to stimulate your mood and keep you up late in the night --- because you KNOW:

- the dawn will come
- the sun will rise
- and it will find you happily underlining the final words that will mark your success and make you a millionaire:

The End~

EVRIKA MAMMA, I MADE IT!!!

Yes. Mno. Bet you just pictured that, didn't you? Now picture this:

You sharpen your pencil, you get a nice cup of coffee to stimulate your mood and keep you up late in the night --- and you turn towards your paper and smile like an idiot. Any moment now. Any moment that brain of yours will start spinning its rusty wheels and start producing quality text. And you keep this on. Keep starring. 10 minutes passed. Your dumb smile fades away. 20 minutes passed. By now you probably have 3 or 4 phrases rephrased 3 or 4 times scribbled all over what used to be a beautiful spotless sheet. You probably blamed your pencil, sharpened it

3 or 4 times. 30 minutes pass by. You finally have a phrase that sounds good. You're so proud you think you deserve another cup of coffee.

You go for a coffee now - smoke a cigarette maybe? Contemplating on how you finally started moving things! From here on everything is going to be like a walk in the park on a sunny day with a mild breeze swiftly dancing around you. You shake your head, you take on a serious face as you realistically realize that storms don't avoid parks. But damn, if it should come, you will be ready.
Then you come back to your desk, you realized 2 hours passed by and you have 1 phrase. Even more, you realize that you don't know how to continue, and frustrated you read that phrase 3 or 4 times more until... you realize it's shit! It's late, you're tired, nothing works - before you know it those wheels in your head spin just enough to get you in bed with some comfort food and some well-deserved Netflix chill-time.

Realistically speaking storms don't hit in-doors, so maybe you need to work on your approach a bit more?

But wait, you're not done.

The carefully placed cherry on top of the cake follows ~ when you yawn, and you decide it's time to call it a night. You shut down your PC, Netflix, TV, whatever. You get cozy in that cozy pajama, jumping in your cozy bed, snuggling your cozy pillow when out of a sudden - it hits you! That brilliant line that brilliant character should cry out in that brilliant scene!

If that line is longer than 5 words, I personally guarantee you, whether you jump from the bed and you go turn your PC on *(it will probably give you a blue screen)* or you give in to the power of sleep thinking you will write it down in the morning --- **you will forget it**. You will remember bits and fragments and when you will try to glue them together you will end up cursing your life because it just doesn't sound as good as it did the first time your head cooked that shit!!

Tip – do yourself a favor and keep your phone close when you sleep.

You might get irradiated and you might get cancer and you might die a slow painful death – but you got that one line!

(Which you will probably lose the next day when you will get robbed of your phone.)

Nonetheless, congratulations, you are an unknown hero of the literature who learned the meaning of a true sacrifice!

Am I right or am I right?

PHASE 4

Phase 4 follows Phase 3. Bet you didn't see that coming did you, Sherlock?

.

.

.

I never made it to Phase 4. Now you're probably laughing an evil laugh thinking *'Karma, you ass-hole!'*

Okay, it's time I come clean and confess. The truth is I am a maniac suffering from depression, anxiety and probably OCD *(all of them self-diagnosed)* upgraded during years with a tormenting feature namely perfectionism, who just wants to write a story and apparently is quite incapable of doing it.

You ready for some dramaaaaa?!

I hope you are because this is where this goes.
About now you probably closed this document.
If not – Congrats!! You can throw your virtual tomatoes and rotten eggs at me and when you're done we can proceed, like normal... grown-ups.

I passed through Phase 1 and 2 and I'm stuck at 3. I've been struggling with 3 for the past few months until I managed to actually bore myself to death *(hence, someone else should suffer with me too, hence you the one reading this --- hiii! How are you enjoying your time in my hell? What's that? Yours is rougher? I don't really care – let's go back to mine.)*. Even today, I am still fighting this weird ass thing so fancily called writer's block, in lack of other terms.

I genuinely thought that maybe I am enchained or constricted by the fact that I imposed myself to actually publish a book and not only write it with the sole purpose of it serving as a cocoon to all the lonely dust particles from my drafts' drawer. Adding it to a drawer where it will probably be abandoned for the next 10 years is not necessarily my definition of purpose in life. Although coming back 10 years later, reading and judging my younger not so talented self while envying the youth I lost across time can make a good laugh/ cry.

STILL - That's been done already. Experience has been experienced.

So.

No. Not anymore. This time I am willing to let strangers do the judging, and use their judging… constructively, because that's what mature people do, more or less. Right? Wrong. Again. I mean maybe. I mean it sounds right, sure, but it never goes according to plan, now does it?
Apparently, this idea of sharing words… proves to be more difficult than I originally anticipated. It forces my perfectionism to reach monstrous limits.

Every damn word I lay on paper seems dull, not interesting, never good enough. Every sentence is either too short or too long. Every phrase is just too boring, and they never seem to catch the essence. Every beginning is a failure that will never catch any reader's interest no matter the reader's patience or expectations.

It just feels wrong.

And then I feel lost. And sad. And I decide to comfort myself with some delicious and sadly quite unhealthy food *(KFC, most likely)*. And then I feel good. And then the food ends and I feel bad again. And I decide to do what any other mortal would do.

Go to thy all know-it-all/all-wise Master Gogu and ask him about the writer's block and he - well he is mighty like that and in his great mercy he decides to take pity on this ravished soul just enough to provide a tone load of shit for me to read.

Varying from *"tips and tricks used to overcome your problem"* to psychological analysis and comforting quotes like *'There, there, it's okay, it happens to all of us!"* - you name it, Gogu has it.

None worked for me.

And the vicious circle kept circling.

On and on and on.

So, I came up with this idea - release all of my writing frustrations into these private pages that probably no one will see or judge *(about now, you roll your eyes thinking it's all been done before, and I roll my eyes thinking shut your brain for a second, it's a waste of calories)*.

And I strongly encourage you to do this as well - keep a journal dedicated to writing only.

And note there everything. Make it messy! Use highlighting markers and doodles and checkboxes and scribble all over the place. Write your grammar mistakes or new words and idioms you learn on the way; write all the good and bad advice and feedback that you receive from either friends or strangers; write it when you feel down and discouraged and write it when you feel positive, content and motivated! Write notes about your characters, your chapters, your timelines; write instant lines that come in your head whenever you expect them the least.

You need this sacred place where you need not to worry about planning any chapters or think of how it sounds. Or that you are repeating yourself and literally make no sense. Whine about everything that you normally wouldn't whine to people because you know that they don't give a rat's ass. Allow yourself to be a spoiled little prick and just write.

Trust me, this is a great way to built your warm-up. Not everyone can write the perfect plot, but everyone has something to complain about.

10 pages ago – when this idea popped in my head, I thought if I'm wrong I will block at the first sentence like I usually do. And yet, so far, I managed to successfully babble for 10 fucking pages. It's been a lifetime since I last managed to write 10 pages. And I keep going at it.

Therefore, the 6th of February 2019, I proudly pronounce this day, the day I passed Phase 3. Guess Karma has a thing for me, eh?

Damn, I feel like a prodigy about now... only... older.

PHASE 5

Wait? What was Phase 4 again? Slap yourself and go back to reading Phase 4 until you get the idea. If you read that 5 times and still don't get it, feel free to quit your writing job. Also, slap yourself again. For my own pleasure and entertainment.

...I hope you know joke and you don't quit. If you don't know joke, or worse, you find my sense of humor doesn't satisfy you, then we got a communication problem here - so feel free to slap yourself unlimitedly until you fix it. I won't stop you.

Where were we?
Yes.
After you write down your frustrations and you throw

some punches and kicks in the air you sit your ass back on that chair and you try again. Or you sit your ass in your bed and you try again, or on the floor, in your bath or on the damn ceiling if you must, and you try again. Use your PC or your laptop, your tablet or your phone or all of them, or a notebook, or just simple plain paper; even your damn toilet paper will do, but you try again.

As a matter of fact, stop reading this crap.

Did you? If you didn't – DO! Take a break and go write something right now.

If you're like:

"Ha, ha, yeah, right. I don't know what to write anyway." – write me a love letter ~

Seriously, love letters are flattering, and I really don't mind. And if you're thinking we might not be compatible as genres, oh God, you're so medieval... Don't worry, it's the 21st century. Trivial things like that can change overnight for the right amount of money ~ ;)

 If you're like:

"I don't have time." – time, my little sloth *(you know what a sloth is, I hope; if you don't please watch Disney's Zootopia)*, is like currency.

And what do we do when we don't have money?

We save it.

So why shouldn't time work the same way? You can save a bit of time from your 2-hour shower, a bit more from your afternoon beauty-sleep, a bit more from watching your favorite TV show, from curling your hair, polishing your nails or cooking your soup.

Baby, we both know that this time problem is the perfect excuse to run away from the things we must do.
You might come now and argue that you're a single mom/dad, you have 2 jobs and 3 children to raise and this time coinage is a luxury you simply can't afford. And I can come and ask you how come you have the time to read this gobbledygook if you're so busy?

But let's not argue.

None of us has time for that.

If you're like:
"I don't feel like it." – just quit. This is not for you. And this time I am mean, and I mean it.

If you're like:
"You can't tell me what to do." – know that I actually can tell you what to do.
You may choose not to listen, and it will probably serve your mental health better. But we both know

that your mental health is already not that stable if you're reading this so:

In case this dude's facial expression and prominent muscles are not convincing enough in a static mode, check the motion version:

https://www.youtube.com/watch?v=ZXsQAXx_ao0

Maybe he is more persuasive than me?

If you're more like:
"I am a free spirit and I will only write what and when my deep sub-conscience will allow it. When my physical mind will be invaded by divine inspiration, I shall then bestow my blessings upon this world and

the world in desperate need of salvation shall turn its face towards what I have to say..."

cricket sounds

... this is beyond my... it's beyond me. Really. Go YOLO, I dunno.

"... and my art shall bring a new dawn of hope over th..."

Okay.
We got it.
Stop.
Next.

Story doesn't want to poop out? Change the file, go back to that journal we talked about earlier and write more frustrations down. Clearly, you're not done yet. If you do this more than 3 times I will judge you. But I don't know who you are so you're free to send me to fuck myself as long as you have the certitude I can't find you and kill you.

Bottom line: those first few sentences/ maybe even first pages/ first love letter for me *(I know you're still thinking about it)* might feel wrong, might sound bad but for the love of Mary Joanna do NOT stop *(unless you're still writing that letter. I won't read it if it's endless.)*.

And then, there's one more thing:

Do not come back and revise your text two thousand times. Take as few short breaks as you can and write as much as you can in one session.

**For the record I am stupid, and I don't follow my own beyond useful advice and hence I am paying dearly with our most precious coin – time. Do not be stupid like me.

But I'm not worrying. You're definitely a smart dude/ dudette and you surely don't listen to strangers, so you will go back and revise over and over and over until you drop back to Phase 3.

sigh

I am not going to repeat myself -> just scroll back up and start over.

No matter how much you like a book you will never read each of its pages 10 times in a row, okay? Why do that to yours then? Why abuse the pages of your notebook or Word or whatever? You brute. Is that how your mamma taught you? *(insert here penguin slap gif. link)*.

PHASE 6

Assuming you passed Phase 5 and gained the knowledge to follow this ever so wise stranger that has made a goal of his merry journey to surpass Master Gogu -

(Yes. Me. Modesty is my second name.)

- You probably managed to let go some of your inhibitions and you feel like you are on the roll!!!
In fact, you're probably convinced you will overcome the world's highest typing speed record ~ little over 200 words per minute, I think?

You can stop reading here. Wasted enough of your precious time. You don't need me anymore. Just add

a thousand $$$ in my account please and we're
done.

Shakes hand.

Arrivederci.

2 days later:

In case you are thinking of asking for a refund.

Hi there. Welcome back. If you're back you're confused. Let's continue.

**About now I am confused too, I think I chose my job wrong, should get a shrink's degree –

Most of the times - unless you suffer from an inflated sense of narcissistic superiority (?) or fear of conspiracy that they all want to steal your ideas, you will probably feel the need to confirm with another party that you are on the right track.
We all need validations, even *me (Hiii~ Miss Veggie ^_^/ Mister Tuby/ Mister Shparkie, wondering if you peep made it this far - for all other readers, please ignore this parenthesis as it serves me more on a personal level)*.

Now. This Phase 6 is a tricky thing. Sharing is caring. In this case, the care is directed mostly towards yourself, so you're not quite a Samaritan. Get over yourself.

First thing - you don't want to hear this, but I don't give a flying ostrich's ass about it: you need to analyze your own ability to receive feedback.

If you have close people you trust *(may God have mercy on them, sorry Veggie/ Tuby/ Shparkie)* is easier. If you don't and you rely mostly on forums and other virtual social interactions *(may God have mercy on you)* well, you need a life.

But don't feel bad, if it helps with anything, I can confirm I need a life too, and so do other 2.5 billion peeps under this Sun. Better?

No?

Eat a Snickers.

Now about the feedback. I have a feeling this might take a while –

How to put this in kind, decent words that don't hurt too much…

Figure it out if you suck or not at it. I know it's not the most delicate way for me to say it, but seriously it's important.

<u>If you are way **too** sensitive to feedback</u> => you can't handle anything else other than *"You're great! It's amazing! O-M-G!! I need so much air, I feel like I can stop breathing when I read your astonishing art!!"* – first, I am not entirely sure how this satisfies you as an artist. But that is not my problem. Not unless you ask

for my feedback in which case… what's the word for a problem that is bigger than a problem? Catastrophe? Let's go with that, has a rough ring to it. Second, the chances for you and I to meet, for you to ask and for me to respond are slimmer than an atom's silhouette.

Even so, your typology is fun to write about and across the entire history of literature, there were a lot of characters inspired and built on a similar foundation. Ultimately, we need to thank the Heavens for your existence. If all of us would be perfect half of the amazing art out there wouldn't be so amazing.

Consequently, as a token of gratitude, heed my advice - DO NOT ask for feedback before you finish up your work. It can be unrefined, but make sure it's done or almost done. Before you start arguing that this doesn't work for you because you are a special snowflake and it just doesn't, take a moment to imagine what follows.

If you don't like where this is going you can stop me anytime.

Haha. I was just funny right now.
You can't really stop me.

Sorry.

You share your pre-refined work with other parties and ask for feedback. The feedback is not what you expected. Your reaction can be described somewhere along these lines: you get upset, you vociferate some weird exasperated obscenities pointing out that they don't understand your level of depth; you casually mention that you're not mad and then you close your chat/ mail/ phone and hang a sign to your door: NOT HOME!
Also, if you read this – you totally don't see yourself in this representation.

Another reaction could be: unwanted feedback totally ruins your mood. Throws you off your balance. If you're a guy, you go get drunk. If you're a girl, you go cry under your blanket. If you're both you probably do both. If you're none, I am sure you'll find something else just as depressing to fill your time with. Point is you are likely to give up and start meditating over how useless your entire existence has been so far. Also, if you read this – you totally find yourself in every word, but you insist on justifying every action you take and refuse change.

About now I am expecting some of you or all of you to think I am a hater.
Fact is I can be.

Spoiler alert* - any of you saw the DC's Titans serial, specifically that scene when Robin hallucinates about meeting his younger self and his younger self beats the crap out of him for all the bad decisions he took? Reverse that and you have me. I would kick my younger self's arse to Moon and back for all those moments of hyper sensibility that dragged me down so many times. I am extremely ashamed to admit but I will admit it because I know it's not a definitive characteristic – you can work with yourself and you can improve as long as you are willing to invest interest and care in the person you want to become.

I manage to deviate by a whole lot - if I bored you take a break to shake it off, go watch some Porn or something and come back after washing your hands.

The thing is - if you know that you are feedback sensitive do not share your **unfinished** work so that you may avoid an unwanted/ unneeded but totally expected outcome. Give yourself the chance to work more, to learn, experiment and evolve.

Share it after you finish up. No matter the end-game feedback you will check at least 2 accomplishments: you finished up a project, which is a lot more than a lot of us ever did, and you gained experience. You will be proud.

You can't quit if you don't know the reactions you trigger, right?

If you are **mildly** sensitive to feedback => bad feedback affects you, sure, you are not a banana, you have feelings! But not enough to put you down, and that is the key here. You are most capable of filtering through other people's opinions, separating what is said out of pure envy or evilness and gathering all the constructive info that you need to continue improving. You sound too perfect, you bore me. I don't want to talk about you anymore.

But before I move on – you are safe to ask for early feedback; it might prove to be quite a tool.

If you are **not** sensitive at all to feedback => you literally don't give a rat's ass about what others have to say and you just continue doing your thing – well

then, you fucking bastard!! Do you even realize the type of blessings the Heavens have bestowed upon you?! Where do you get your genes from? Can I have a child with you? I'm sure he will be a prodigy!
It's pretty self-explanatory why you shouldn't ask for feedback, but if you're an ass and you just want to consume people's time for your own delight, by all means, please proceed.

One short note before we end Phase 6. Remember when we mentioned the conspiracy of stealing ideas?
Don't be paranoiac about that but don't treat it too leisurely either. Whether we like to admit it or not sh*t happens.

PHASE 7

Let's recap a bit.

You came up with an idea.

You decided to share it with the world because deifying yourself is not that exciting and you need to breathe in other minions' worshipping.

You had some problems finding the right words to trigger the addiction in your future followers but eventually, you decided to work on your text's hallucinogenic effect after you're done with the actual text.

Hats off, I am so proud of you – oh, how you've grown! <3

You passed the first mile and maybe asked for some feedback that you used fruitfully further on.

Unless you know for sure what happens with your characters from the beginning until the end, my guess is the next difficulty you will have a hot date with is thy Grande Finale. Even more, if this is your first try on taking on a challenge of writing a story.

If you think your biggest problem is your imag-ination as it generates endless possibilities of endings, besides the fact that I feel like shooting you, I can also tell you in a polite manner that your problem is your inflamed brain. You should check it, maybe you had a stroke. Too much imagination can never be a problem in this line of work.

You have too many possible endings? You can't decide? Write them all down. It's never a waste of time to write something down even if you will end up discarding 100 pages after you're thru.

You wrote them down and you adore every one of them so much you still can't decide? Ask for another feedback. And if that doesn't work either maybe it's a sign you should keep them all. Maybe your story is so good that you will get an offer for a multiple-choice based game or graphic novel project collaboration *(it's kind of a thing these days, a thing I also am into).*

Can you imagine someone taking your char-acters and literally bringing them to life through images and videos or 3D rendering and giving them a real voice?

Of course you can imagine, that's what Phase 1 was all about ~ :D

So, you don't need me to tell you it'd be a fucking waste not to write all those endings down!!

On the other hand, if you just don't know how to end things – you are probably thinking you can find your inspiration by shooting the ones that know too many ways and protest about it. I feel you, bro, but murder is not the answer. Excruciating torture is. Still, for now, leave them and let's talk about you a bit.

You will need to arm yourself with a lot of patience because you are not going to like this. If you know it's time to wrap things up and you don't know how, and you know you tried everything and nothing worked - **take a break.** You're probably confused asking yourself:

"Wait! What?! What happened to hanging my ass on the ceiling and writing on toilet paper just to get it done?"

That was then. This is now.

As you approach the finish line you will become impatient and use a massive amount of energy to cross it *(kind of like a marathon when you spent your every bit of last energy to push through that last 100 meters distance)*.

You might feel tempted to just round off and be done with it.

Halt.

Rushing the end can and will ruin your entire work if done poorly.

Lay low for like let's say a month or more? And then come back and with fresh eyes read your chapters from start to end like you would read someone else's.

Sometimes this simple but time-consuming method can work miracles.

It should feel like that moment when you grab a book/movie and read/ see through half of it and you start imagining how it will end. What would sound more like be a predictable outcome and what could sincerely surprise you?

If you're like me though, you have another problem. Most likely psychological. You just don't want to end anything and each time you get close to a potential ending you twist your plot to 180 degrees to evade it. You probably created your own fictional world where you can escape to avoid those irritatingly real day-to-day problems – which means you would have to be masochistic to terminate it or on a more positive note, to find that genuine happiness in life that everyone's searching for.

This is good if you want to write a sexlogy *(not sexology, okay? sexlogy, like trilogy, but with six instead of three; and yes I do know that word doesn't exist, but it's still fun to imagine you arguing about it, you little squint)* or something and there is a tone of people out there who can effectively use this skill set.

Sadly, I am not one of them. My ability to create suspense and intrigue without touching a cringe extreme is not something I find myself capable of doing, so far. And since I haven't managed to pass this point obviously I have no idea what I am doing so I will refrain from rambling any further.
If I ever find a pertinent answer I will make sure not to tell anyone and keep it to myself. If I find an impertinent one, we will discuss it in Volume II.

PHASE 8

We are slowly approaching the end. It's been a long journey and I lost the count on how many days I wasted on this thing and the mood to waste any more *(remember that finish line we talked about? yah, it's happening)*.

How do you feel? Don't bother answering. If I'd really care I'd give you my phone and listen to you chattin' about it but you didn't care enough to write me a letter so go suck a carrot.

You're finally done. You're exhausted. But there is a sense of fulfillment you really didn't felt before – you can go spoil yourself with some deep fried spicy chicken or cheesy pasta/ or better yet a fine stake and an expensive bottle of wine *(because you're not depressed anymore)* and just breathe for a second.

Second past, let's go back to work.

It's that time when you are finally allowed to revise your writing and see what else you can do/ add or remove to make it better.

Don't overdo it.

Don't exaggerate with your search for syno-nyms/ antonyms/ idioms/ expressions that are way too fancy or sophisticated – they will give you a fake sense of *professionalism (especially if don't know how to use them correctly)* and I guarantee you - not even you will remember their meaning the next day.

You don't want your readers to squeeze the dictionary when reading your stuff.

You don't want to squeeze the dictionary when you read your stuff 10 years from now.

Gather all your head titles if you have any and pin down your Content page. It's also that time when you can have you share of fun playing with the page format and fonts and everything else that gives you that feeling that is finally starting to look like a book *(I really thought this is going to be fun, but really... is not fun at all).*

Add the Cover if you must, save it as a PDF and:
Boom!
You're done.
Easy enough?
Now what?
Now… it's no longer my business.

^ Kind of sounds like a rushed and poor ending, eh? Now you understand what I mean? I hope this has been traumatic enough to leave a mark and remind you how NOT to finish your book.

Nop.

Nothing here.

That was literally it.

F.A.Q

<u>*What the hell did I just read? What is this crap?*</u>

I'm glad you ask.

This is me facing Phase 4 and all its tricky trials. I am releasing and sealing my demons into these pages so that I can finally move on to Phase 5. Consider me and these sheets as your personal guinea pig and his piggish sheets – most of what has been said here has been experimented while it was being said resulting in this "crap" you asked about.

<u>*Who the heck did you say you are?*</u>

Nobody.

I don't have the experience of a writer who published

200 works.

I am not a Youtuber. I am not a blogger.

I don't have a psychology degree.

For you, I don't have a face and I don't have a name.

All I have is what you read.

Nothing more. Nothing less.

Why should that interest you? Mostly, it shouldn't.

However, if a day comes when you feel like you need a slap in your head to help you get your shit together, read these pages and remember someone else out there, in this vast and cold world, needs that slap as bad as you do.

Afterwards, you can imagine I'm slapping your head like Gibs/Leroy Jethro slaps Tony DiNozzo in NCIS each time he says/does something stupid *(search it, I know you want too – NCIS All Gibbs' Head slaps Seasons 1 - 12)*.

<u>*Okay. You're weird. But why?*</u>

Because of Phase 3, why else?

I, too, want to write a book, a psychological/ thriller/

romance novel, superior to all other psychological/ thriller/ romance novels out there.

I couldn't stop thinking about how I have this whole storyline all set and waiting for me to just bring it to life.

Had it all – how it should begin, what should happen and towards what type of end it should lead. And yet, each time I opened a new Word document I froze.

So, I had to find a workaround, a way to move past my previous defeats and all my meaningless obstructions. I opened a word document and started writing about...writing. Because that was my problem. And because my problem needed a solution. And I hoped to find it as ideas come easier when I write about them.

**If you were asking me why I am weird – know that I am still asking myself that every day too.

<u>Did it work?</u>

Partially, no.

As I continued to pass through these Phases, I became impatient to finish this masterpiece *(Phase 7, right? We talked about this.)*, and I postponed finishing my other project once more.

Partially, yes.

I am not bored anymore.

Ideas flow effortlessly in my head and my Word-phobia's levels dropped significantly. We call that progress, eh? You should try it too!

Will it help me?

I am not Nostradamus.

If you reached this page there is a 99% chance you already know the answer.

...

You're welcome.

THE END ~

You've made it this far and about now you're
probably grinning and thinking to yourself what a
major waste of time and how this son of a donkey
managed to bull*hit you enough to spare 2$ ~
(Why thank you, sugar! ::*:* Your compliment is*
accepted! Your $ is appreciated too, I'll make sure
not to waste it).

Yours truly,
Za-ar Twist

www.ingramcontent.com/pod-product-compliance
Lightning Source LLC
Chambersburg PA
CBHW040232240726
48664CB00001B/100